A New True Book

GREECE

By Karen Jacobsen

CHILDRENS PRESS ®
CHICAGO

The Acropolis of Athens

PHOTO CREDITS

The Bettmann Archive—33 (2 photos)

The Marilyn Gartman Agency—© Christy Volpe, 13 (left), 17 (bottom left)

© Virginia Grimes—39 (left)

Reprinted with permission of *The New Book of Knowledge*, 1989 edition, © Grolier Inc.—5 (top)

Historical Pictures Service, Chicago—24, 25, 30 (2 photos)

Journalism Services—© Gill S. J. Copeland, 5 (bottom left)

North Wind Picture Archives—15 (right), 27 (2 photos), 28

Odyssey Productions—© Robert Frerck, 16 (right)

Photri—7 (left), © D. J. Dianellis, 2, 8, 17 (right); © B. Kulik, 45 (bottom left)

Root Resources—© Russel A. Kriete, 39 (right); © Mrs. Jane H. Kriete, 44 (left)

Shostal Associates/SuperStock International, Inc.—9 (left), 15 (left), 40 (left and right), 41 (left), 44 (right), 45 (top left); © Konstantinos Koroneos, 40 (center) 45 (bottom center)

SuperStock International, Inc.—Cover, 10, 17 (top left), 45 (top right)

Tony Stone Worldwide/Click-Chicago—14; © Suzanne & Nick Geary, 5 (bottom right); © Deborah Revell, 9 (right); © Berlitz, 21 (bottom left); © Brian Seed, 37 (bottom left)

Third Coast Stock Source—© Paul H. Henning, 16 (left); © Phil Krejcarek, 22 (right); © Thomas Lemke, 37 (bottom right), 42 (left); © Peter Baker, 41 (right)

UPI/Bettmann Newsphotos—34

Valan—© Aubrey Diem, 11 (2 photos), 18 (right); © Kennon Cooke, 21 (top left), 22 (left), 37 (top left and right), 42 (right)

© Jerome Wyckoff, 13 (right), 19

Len W. Meents maps—7 (right), 18 (left)

Cover: Mykonos — one of the Greek Islands

Library of Congress Cataloging-in-Publication Data

Jacobsen, Karen.
    Greece / by Karen Jacobsen.
        p.   cm. — (A New true book)
    Includes index.
    Summary: Examines the geography, history, and modern life of Greece.
    ISBN 0-516-01185-5
    1. Greece—Juvenile
literature. [1. Greece.] I. Title.
DF717.J33   1990   89-25343
949.5—dc20   CIP
                                                    AC

TABLE OF CONTENTS

THE LAND

Greece lies on the edge of
Europe. It is close to two other
continents. It shares its
eastern border with Asia, and
is across the Mediterranean
Sea from Africa.

People have been living in
Greece for more than five
thousand years.

The country of Greece has
thousands of islands and
dozens of peninsulas. Its
mainland is nearly 365 miles

GREECE

Greece's many islands are dotted with small villages.

long and 343 miles wide.
The Greek mainland is part
of the Balkan Peninsula.

Other countries on the
Balkan Peninsula are
Albania, Yugoslavia,
Bulgaria, and the western
part of Turkey. The Balkan
countries are alike in many
ways. But they are not
friends. A long history of war
and hatred has made them
bitter enemies.

A valley in Central Greece

THE MAINLAND PROVINCES

On the mainland of
Greece there are several
large provinces. Thrace,
Macedonia, and Epirus are
in the north. Thessaly and
Central Greece are in the
middle. The Peloponnesus is
in the south.

7

The province of Thrace shares a border with Turkey in the east. Along its northern border lie the Rhodope Mountains.

Much of Thrace is covered with hills and mountains. It has only a few small towns

Small villages are found along Greece's long shoreline.

Greek farmers (left) harvest crops. The windmill (above) pumps water for irrigation.

and not many people. On its coastal plain, by the Aegean Sea, farmers grow crops of tobacco, grains, and cotton. Lignite (brown coal) is mined in Thrace.

Macedonia is the province west of Thrace and south of Yugoslavia. It too has many

9

A plateau in mainland Greece

hills and mountains. Along its coastal plain, farmers raise livestock and crops of cotton, fruits, rice, tobacco, and wheat.

Salonika, the second largest city in Greece, is in

Salonika is a hilly port city in northern Greece.

Macedonia. It is a busy port situated on the Aegean Sea. Salonika is also a center for manufacturing. Electric power plants burn lignite to produce electricity for use in many parts of Greece.

The Pindus Mountains in Epirus Province are over 8,000 feet high. They run north to south, dividing Epirus from Macedonia— and from the rest of Greece. To the north of Epirus are more mountains and the country of Albania.

Because there are so many mountains, there are few roads in Epirus. The best way to travel is by boat on the Ionian Sea.

The lower slopes of the mountains provide good

The Ionian Sea (left) has many small islands. The Pindus Mountains (right) divide Epirus from Macedonia.

grass for feeding horses, cattle, sheep, and goats.

Sawmills at Kalambak turn trees from the forests of Epirus into lumber for shipment to other parts of Greece.

Thessaly is a large province. It has the best

13

farmland in Greece.
Because of its great wheat
crop it is often called the
"breadbasket of Greece." Its
other important crops are
olives, sugar beets, fruits,
and vegetables.

A town in Thessaly

Mount Olympus (left) once was thought to be the home of Zeus (above) and the other Greek gods and goddesses.

Mount Olympus in the north of Thessaly is the highest peak in Greece. In ancient times, people believed that Zeus, the king of the gods, and the other gods in his family lived in palaces on the top of Mount Olympus.

15

Athens is crowded with modern apartment buildings and city traffic.

Central Greece is home to more than a third of Greece's people. Its largest city is Athens. More than three million people live in or near Athens. It is the center of government and business for all of Greece.

The Parthenon (top left) and an ancient temple (above) to the goddess Athena, stand on the Acropolis of Athens. The busy port of Piraeus (left)

Athens is the site of some of the oldest ruins on earth. Piraeus is the seaport of Athens. From Piraeus, ships travel to ports of call all over the world.

Corinth Canal

THE PELOPONNESUS

The peninsula of the Peloponnesus is shaped like a large four-fingered hand. Patras is the largest city on the peninsula.

Once ships had to sail around the Peloponnesus. But in 1857 a canal was dug at Corinth. Now, ships sail

The athletes at Olympia ran under this arch when they entered the stadium.

through the Corinth Canal.

The Peloponnesus has many ancient ruins. The most famous is at Olympia. Long ago, in 776 B.C., Greek athletes met at Olympia to test their skills at the first Olympic Games.

19

THE GREEK ISLANDS

Thousands of islands surround the Greek mainland. The Ionian Islands are in the west. The Aegean Islands are in the east. To the south, in the Mediterranean Sea, lies Crete, the largest Greek island.

Ionian Islands

Aegean Islands

Patras Corinth Athens
Mycenae
Nauplion

Crete

Windmills are used for irrigation in Crete.

Greek crafts include wood carving (top left)
and weaving (bottom left).
Fishermen (above) pull in their nets.

The people who live on
the islands may work as
farmers or fishermen or boat
builders. Others may make
shoes or bake bread. Many
people run restaurants or
rent rooms to tourists.

21

Minoan vases (left) and the ruins of the palace at Knossos, Crete (right)

ANCIENT GREECE

On the island of Crete, there are ruins dating from about 1400 B.C. They are the remains of the Minoan people. The Minoans were skillful builders and artists.

Their ships traded with other Mediterranean countries.

The Minoan civilization ended when other Aegean people destroyed the city of Knossos.

Over the next thousand years, Greek villages fought one another and outside invaders. Some of the villages grew to be large city-states. Sparta, Corinth, and Argos were powerful city-states, but Athens was the greatest of all.

Athens was the center of

The Acropolis looked like this in ancient times.
The Parthenon is at the upper right.

democracy. Its citizens were the first people in the world to vote for their own leaders. Athens was also the center for trade, learning, and art. Its great architects built magnificent temples.

PHILIP II AND ALEXANDER THE GREAT

Alexander the Great

By 338 B.C., the army of Philip II of Macedonia conquered the city-states.

Alexander, the son of Philip II, later led the Greek army against the Persian Empire to the east. He defeated the Persians and, for a short time, was head of

25

the largest empire the world had ever known.

But Alexander died in 323 B.C. His empire broke up. For a while, the Greeks ruled their own cities.

In 146 B.C., Greece became a province of the Roman Empire. Its new name was Achaea.

The Roman Empire was larger than Alexander's empire. In A.D. 330, the Emperor Constantine moved the capital from Rome to the eastern city of

The Emperor Constantine (left) made Constantinople the new capital of the Roman Empire.

Byzantium. He renamed the city Constantinople. Achaea was now a part of the East Roman, or Byzantine, Empire. The Byzantine Empire held together for almost one thousand years.

THE OTTOMAN TURKS

In the 1300's, the Ottoman Turks attacked and took over Greece and most of the Byzantine Empire. They completed the takeover in 1453, when they captured the city of Constantinople. The Turks would rule Greece for four hundred years.

The victorious Ottoman Turks took over Constantinople in 1453.

INDEPENDENCE

In the early 1800's, many Greek patriots wanted to win freedom for Greece.

In 1821, an army of Greeks drove the Turks out of the Peloponnesus, Athens, and some of the Aegean Islands.

But, four years later, the Turks returned. The bloody war dragged on, and neither side could win.

Finally, the three most powerful nations in Europe—

Otto of Bavaria

King George I

Britain, France, and Russia —
forced an end to the war and
made the Turks leave.

In 1833, the European
powers made Prince Otto of
Bavaria the king of Greece.
This made the Greek patriots
very unhappy.

The Greeks kept trying to
get rid of Otto and form their
own government.

In 1862, Otto left Greece. The Greeks chose George I, a Danish prince, to be the new Greek king.

In 1864, a new Constitution limited the king's power and set up an elected Parliament. At last, the Greek leaders would have a chance to govern the kingdom of Greece.

In 1913, after a war with the Ottoman Turks, Greece was given the territories of Crete, Epirus, Macedonia, and the Aegean Islands.

In June of 1917, Greece entered World War I on the side of Britain, France, and the United States.

In 1921, the Greeks and Turks fought over the land south of Bulgaria. Many Greeks lived there under Turkish rule.

In 1923, the European powers decided to move the 1,250,000 Greeks living under Turkish rule to Greece and send the 400,000 Turks in Greece to Turkey. It was hoped that if all the Greeks

were in Greece, there wouldn't
be any reason for them to go
to war with the Turks again.

By 1936, there was a
worldwide depression. The
king, George II, allowed
General Joannes Metaxas to
become the military dictator
of Greece.

King George II

General Joannes Metaxas

When World War II began, Greece tried to stay out of the war. But, in 1940, Italy attacked. Metaxas and the Greek army drove the Italians out of Greece.

In 1941, the German army occupied Greece. Many Greeks lived in the mountains and attacked the Germans.

The German army invading Greece in 1941

Finally, in 1944, the Germans left Greece. Greek Communists tried to take over. But George II returned to fight the Communists. The civil war continued. Finally, the Communists were defeated in 1949.

Since the end of World War II, Greece has had two kings, four prime ministers, a military junta, and, at times, no government at all. Today a prime minister heads the government.

GREECE TODAY

Greece has very little fertile farmland and even less woodland. Its climate is hot and dry. But Greek farmers raise enough food to feed the Greek people.

Greece has few natural resources. Its most useful minerals are lignite and bauxite (aluminum). Also, Greek marble is used to make buildings and statues in Greece and other countries.

Tourists come to see splendid ancient ruins
and to buy the beautiful Greek handicrafts.

Greece's two most
important industries are
tourism and shipping.

37

Textile-weaving, chemical-processing, and metal-refining are other fast-growing industries.

Greek children start school at six years of age. The elementary school, called "demotilo," has six grades. The "gymnacio," or middle school, follows with three grades. Students must pass a special examination to go on to high school.

Greek public schools are free. Students who pass the

Greek schoolchildren
visiting the Parthenon.
Athens University (above)

required tests may attend a
free public university.

In Greece more than 90
percent of the people can
read and write. More than
half of Greece's people live
on islands or in the country.

In Greece, it is the
custom to wear black

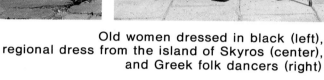
Old women dressed in black (left),
regional dress from the island of Skyros (center),
and Greek folk dancers (right)

clothing to show respect for
dead relatives. Many Greek
people wear black all the
time, for most of their lives.

Each region of Greece has
its own costume. Many are
decorated with gold coins
and rich embroidery. People
wear these costumes for

A costume worn on the island
of Corfu (left); Greek Orthodox priests
(above) lead a religious procession.

special events and holidays.
Almost all Greeks belong
to the Greek Orthodox Church.
The holy days are holidays.
Christmas and Easter are
two important holy days.
Greeks also celebrate many
saints' days.

41

On holidays, schools and businesses close. People go to church and then eat holiday foods. Weddings and christenings are celebrated with parties. Everyone eats, drinks, and dances.

Greek meals are richly

Many kinds of olives (below) are grown and sold in Greece. A Greek buffet (right) featuring meat and seafood.

flavored and hearty. They
are made with fish, meats,
cheeses, vegetables, and
fruits that are native to
Greece.

The ancient Greeks held
great sporting contests
called olympiads.

Modern Greeks still
practice many of the ancient
sports. But they also play
soccer and basketball. Many
Greek athletes are excellent
swimmers, divers, and sailors.

In ancient times, Greek
writers created plays called

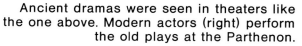
Ancient dramas were seen in theaters like the one above. Modern actors (right) perform the old plays at the Parthenon.

dramas that told about the actions and problems of kings, heroes, gods, and goddesses. Dramas were performed in huge outdoor theaters.

Today, these ancient

Greek dramas are performed

The people of Greece reflect the mixture of old and new.

in modern languages around the world.

Life in Greece is a mixture of old and new. People live in the present, but they are surrounded by the past. No matter what, life goes on. For Greeks, life is good.

45

WORDS YOU SHOULD KNOW

Africa(AF • rih • ka) — the large continent south of Europe

ancient(AIN • shent) — of very great age, from a long time ago

architect(AR • kih • tekt) — building designer

Asia(AIJ • uh) — the largest continent on earth; has the Pacific Ocean on the east and Europe on the west

border(BOR • der) — edge, boundary

capital(KAP • ih • tal) — city where a country's government is located

citizen(SIT • ih • zen) — a legal inhabitant of a place

city-state(SIT • ee • STAIT) — a large town with its own government

climate(KLY • mit) — the usual weather conditions in a place

Communist(KAHM • yoo • nist) — a person who believes in Communism, which requires the common ownership of all property

Constitution(kahn • stih • TOO • shun) — a document of laws for a government

continent(KON • tih • nent) — one of seven large landmasses on Earth

costume(KAHSS • toom) — special type of clothing from a region, a time period, or an occupation

custom(KUH • stum) — tradition, usual practice, habit

democracy(dih • MOCK • rah • see) — government by the people

depression(dee • PRESH • uhn) — a time when business activity is slow

dictator(DIK • tay • ter) — person who rules with absolute power

drama(DRAH • mah) — a play acted on a stage

embroidery(em • BROY • der • ee) — designs stitched with thread and needle

enemy(EN • ih • mee) — a dangerous or unfriendly person or nation

Europe(YOO • rup) — a continent north of Africa and west of Asia

examination(egg • zam • ih • NAY • shun) — a test of knowledge

fertile(FUR • til) — capable of growing crops

govern(GUV • ern) — to manage or control

independent(in • dih • PEN • dint) — not controlled by another person or country

junta(HUN • tah) — an assembly for making laws, usually not elected

mainland(MAYN • land) — large area of land near the sea

military(MILL • ih • tair • ee) — organization of soldiers, troops

modern(MAHD • ern) — being up-to-date; recent

Parliament(PAR • lih • ment) — an elected body of representatives who make laws

patriot(PAY • tree • ut) — person who supports his or her native land or government

peninsula(pen • IN • soo • luh) — a piece of land almost surrounded by water and connected to a larger body of land

plain(PLAYN) — a flat land area

province(PRAHV • ince) — a state or section of a country

quarry(KWOR • ee) — to cut stone out of the earth

ruins(ROO • ins) — the remains of buildings

site(SYTE) — place, location

skill(SKIL) — great ability

temple(TEM • pil) — a house of worship

INDEX

About the Author

Karen Jacobsen is a graduate of the University of Connecticut and Syracuse University. She has been a teacher and is a writer. She likes to find out about interesting subjects and then write about them.